D1450970

Samson the
Strong Man

Copyright © 1993 by Hunt & Thorpe

All rights reserved. Written permission must be secured from the
publisher to use or reproduce any part of this book, except for
brief quotations in critical reviews or articles.

Published in Nashville, Tennessee, by Oliver-Nelson Books, a
division of Thomas Nelson, Inc., Publishers, and distributed in
Canada by Lawson Falle, Ltd., Cambridge, Ontario.

Printed in Malaysia

Library of Congress Cataloging-in-Publication Data

Pipe, Rhona.
Samson the strong man/Rhona Pipe; illustrated by Jenny Press.
p. cm. — (Now I can read Bible stories)
Summary: A simple retelling of the Bible story of Samson and how
he lost his great strength.
ISBN 0-8407-3421-2
1. Samson (Biblical judge) — Juvenile literature. 2. Bible
stories, English — O.T. Judges. [1. Samson (Biblical judge)
2. Bible stories — O.T.]. I. Press, Jenny. ill. II. Title.
III. Series.
BS580-S15P56 1992
222′.3209505 — dc20

92-13326
CIP
AC

1 2 3 4 5 6 — 98 97 96 95 94 93

Samson the Strong Man

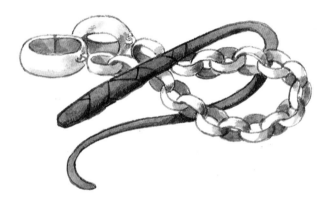

Rhona Pipe

Illustrated by
Jenny Press

THOMAS NELSON PUBLISHERS
Nashville

"The sea people are coming.
Quick! Hide!
They want our food and sheep.
They want to kill us!"
God's people were scared
of the sea people.

Manoah's wife was sad.
She did not have a child.
One day God sent an angel to her.
"God will give you a son,"
the angel said.
"Your son will help to set
your people free.
He will belong to God.
Do not cut his hair."

Samson grew up very strong.
Once he killed a lion
with his bare hands!
One day he lost his temper.
He killed a lot of sea people.
He began a war.
The sea people were scared
of Samson.

The sea people wanted to kill Samson.
But Samson was too strong.
Then Samson fell in love
with Delilah.
"Find out what makes
Samson strong,"
the sea people said.
"We will pay you well, Delilah."

"Samson, what could make you weak?"
Delilah asked.

"Tie me up with seven new strings,"
Samson joked.

Wrong.

"Don't tease me,"
Delilah said.

"What will make you weak?"

"Tie me with brand new ropes."

Wrong.

"Come on," Delilah said.
"Tell me."
"Weave seven strands of my
hair in your loom."
Wrong.
"If you love me, then tell me.
Tell me!" Samson gave in.
"My long hair shows I trust God,"
he said.
Delilah told the sea people
Samson's secret.

Samson fell asleep.

His head was on Delilah's lap.

The sea people cut off his hair.

"Samson! Samson!

The sea people are here!"

Delilah said.

Samson woke up and said,

"I will get free all right."

But Samson did not know

God had left him.

He was weak.

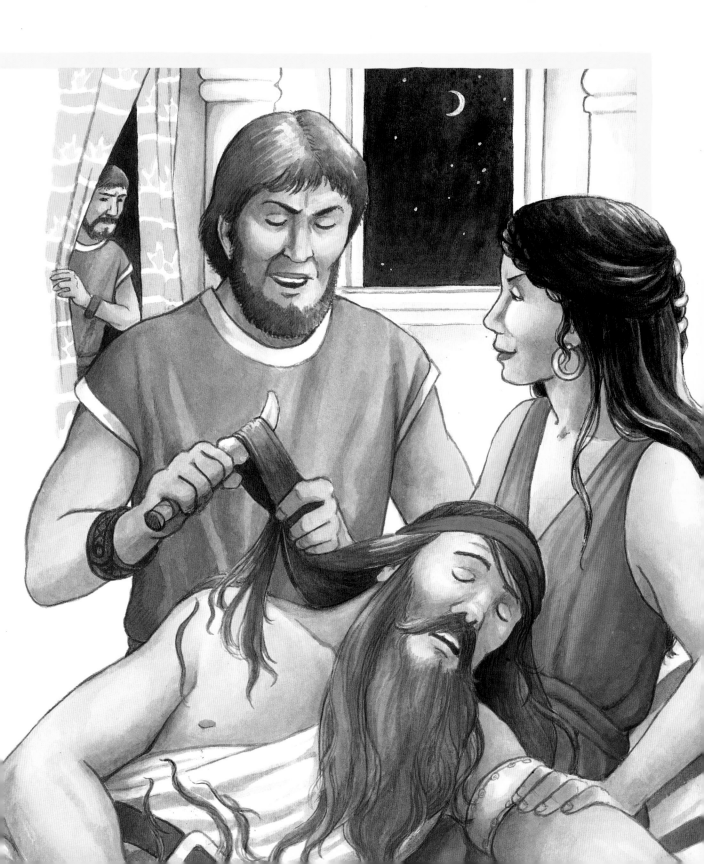

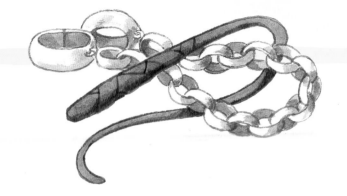

The sea people got Samson.
They put him in chains.
They put out his eyes.
They made blind Samson walk
round and round.
He had to pull a rope to grind corn.
His hair began to grow out.
And Samson cried to God for help.

The sea people held a party
for their god.
They got Samson and made him
do tricks for them.
Two posts held up the temple.
Samson stood between them.
"God, make me strong again,"
Samson prayed. "Then let me die."
And he pushed the posts.

Down came the posts.
Down came the temple.
Down came all the sea people.
All their leaders were killed.
And Samson died happy.
He had trusted God again.
He had helped to set
his people free.